10/03

piercing
prOverbs

piercing prOverbs

melody carlson

Multnomah® Publishers *Sisters, Oregon*

PIERCING PROVERBS
published by Multnomah Publishers, Inc.
and in association with the literary agency of Sara A. Fortenberry

© 2002 by Melody Carlson
International Standard Book Number: 1-57673-895-7

Cover design by David Carlson Design
Cover image by Steven Puetzer/Photonica

Unless otherwise noted, all Scripture references are the author's own paraphrase.
Other Scripture quotations are from: *The Holy Bible,* New Living Translation (NLT)
© 1996. Used by permission of Tyndale House Publishers, Inc.
All rights reserved.

For information:
MULTNOMAH PUBLISHERS, INC. · P.O. BOX 1720 · SISTERS, OR 97759

Library of Congress Cataloging-in-Publication Data

Carlson, Melody.
    Piercing Proverbs / by Melody Carlson.
        p. cm.
Summary: Presents a selection of paraphrased Proverbs, chosen for their
relevance to the lives of modern teens.
    ISBN 1-57673-895-7
    1. Bible. O.T. Proverbs—Meditations. 2. Teeenagers—Religious life. 3. Christian
life. [1. Bible. O.T. Proverbs—Meditations. 2. Prayer books and devotions.
3. Christian life.] I. Title.
    BS1465.4 .C37 2002
    248.8'3—dc21

                                                    2001006383

02 03 04 05 06 07 08 09—10 9 8 7 6 5 4 3 2 1 0

Table of Contents

Introduction: What This Is   7

1. Finding God   9

2. Don't Be a Fool   17

3. Don't Hang with a Fool   25

4. Watch Your Words   33

5. Wisdom Hunt   41

6. The Good Life   47

7. Good Friends   53

8. Family Stuff   59

9. A Handle on Money   65

10. Guard Your Heart   71

11. Keep the Faith   79

Taking Proverbs Another Step   85

What This Is

Are you looking for something more in your life? New meaning, fresh challenges—something that really hits you right where you live?

There's an ancient book in the Bible that's full of real answers, real help, and real advice for *real* people. It's the book of Proverbs (found right smack in the middle of your Bible). Maybe you've read from it before but didn't quite get it. Or maybe it didn't seem to relate to *your* life, *your* questions, *your* problems. Things like severe peer pressure, drugs, alcohol, tough questions about dating and sexuality—real stuff that happens in real life.

This book, written in today's language, invites you—a real teenager living in the real world—to hear and learn from the extreme wisdom found in Proverbs.

. . . for wisdom will enter your heart, and knowledge will fill you with joy.
PROVERBS 2:10, NLT

Listen to me and treasure my instructions.
Tune your ears to wisdom, and concentrate on understanding.
Cry out for insight and understanding.
Search for them as you would for lost money or
    hidden treasure.
Then you will understand what it means to fear the LORD,
And you will gain knowledge of God.

Proverbs 2:1–5 NLT

Let listen to the instructions. Turn your ears to wisdom.

Listen to Him

If you listen to God and hang onto His every word like it's worth more than a winning lottery ticket, then you'll start to figure out and begin to know what's really true–and what's not. And then you will find God! PROVERBS 2:1-5

Have you ever heard God speak to you? Can you recognize His voice? Do you know how to listen to His Word?

God speaks to us in a variety of ways. For instance, you can read God's Word for yourself in the Bible. Or you can experience it when someone teaches from Scripture. Or He might speak to you through song lyrics, a friend's wise advice, or a parent's warning. And if you're really tuned in to God, you can even hear Him whisper right into your heart. *But do you always listen?* For, as everyone knows, hearing and listening aren't really the same thing.

Say you're out snowboarding and you hear someone say, "Better stay off the south side today. There's avalanche danger!" Even though you *hear* the warning, you decide not to *listen*, 'cause it's a pretty cool ride on the south side. And before you know it, you're heading straight for disaster. All because you didn't listen—you didn't take those words seriously.

The same is true with the Bible. Often we hear His Word, but we choose not to listen—not to take it to heart. We decide to go our own way instead. And where does it get us?

But when we really tune in to God's Word and listen to what He's telling us, and when we really start to grasp how totally valuable it is to our lives, that's when we start to understand what's really good for us and what's not. That's when we start making smart choices. And that's when we really find God and begin to experience an awesome and vital relationship with Him.

Long for Him

If you start to understand with your heart, not just your head, and if you really long to know what God is telling you, and if you want His truth so badly that you're willing to scream out loud: "I'm begging You, God, please tell me what's going on!" then you will find Him. PROVERBS 2:2, 5

Have you ever wanted something so badly that you were willing to make a total fool of yourself just to get it? Can you imagine yourself running around, just yelling and screaming—with everyone staring at you? Sounds pretty crazy, doesn't it?

But what if it was a matter of life and death? Like what if you were trapped inside a burning building and didn't know how to get out? I bet you'd yell and scream then. 'Cause when the stakes are high, we don't worry much about looking stupid anymore. At that point, we don't care what others think of us.

And yet knowing and understanding God's direction for

our lives *is* about life and death. Because only God can show us the best way to go and the best way to live. Only He has the answers to all of our toughest questions. So maybe we need to get a little radical in our search for His answers. Maybe we need to be willing to look slightly foolish in order to know His ways and understand Him better.

God tells us that if we cry out to Him, He *will* answer. If we seek Him with all we've got, He *will* show Himself. So what are we waiting for? Let's really get out there in our search for God. Let's be willing to take risks and ask God those tough questions. Because that's when we'll find Him, and that's when we'll experience a real and vital relationship with Him.

Speak to Him

If you're not afraid to question things and to speak up and if you can say: "I want to know what's really real. I want to know what's really crucial for my life!" and if you want this more than you want the latest DVD player, more than a skateboard or a brand-new Maserati, and if you're willing to search long and hard, you will find Him! PROVERBS 2:3-5

Do you really think you can rock God's boat? I mean is there anything you can possibly say or do that will startle or shock or even offend Him? Of course not! He's heard and seen it all. Just read the Old Testament and see for yourself the kind of crazy stuff God has witnessed man do. It's time to accept that there's absolutely nothing we can say or question or suggest that is too much for His ears. He's unshakable.

And the plain fact is that God's just waiting for us to speak up. He desperately wants us to come to Him and tell Him *everything*. He wants us to ask Him the toughest questions. And He wants us to long for His answers and His truth more than we long for anything else on this entire planet.

So think about it: What would you like more than anything? And be honest. Wouldn't you just love to win a million bucks? Or a really cool car? How about a prepaid credit card with an unlimited balance? Naturally, all those things sound pretty cool. But what if we wanted God more than we wanted those other things? What if knowing Him and really understanding Him were worth more than anything to us?

And what if you put as much time and energy into seeking God as you put into getting whatever object you think you want more than anything right now? Think about it: *What if you wanted God more?* Because when you do—when you value Him above all else—that's when everything in your life falls into order. And that's when life begins to make sense. Only then can you really find God, and when you do, you realize that He's worth more than anything and everything this world can offer!

The godly speak words that are helpful, but the wicked speak only what is corrupt.

PROVERBS 10:32, NLT

Experience Him!

For then you'll be ready to see God for who He really is and you'll begin to know and experience Him. And that's when you'll start to understand what He's really all about. PROVERBS 2:5

Have you ever actually seen God with your own eyes? Is it even possible? We understand that He's a spiritual being—so wouldn't He be too huge, too awesome, too totally incredible, to be seen with our mere earthly eyes? And besides, wouldn't it just blow our minds to really see Him? I mean, how could we ever see anything again—at least, in the same way?

And yet we *can* experience God's presence in thousands of ways. Like we see His creativity displayed in nature every day—trees, flowers, animals, newborn babies. And just watch a group of mischievous monkeys—or your friends in the cafeteria—and you'll see God's humor at work. And, of course, we can witness His magnificent glory in a majestic mountain peak, a colorful sunset, or the thundering surf of the sea.

So He does reveal Himself to us in lots of ways—but we only see Him if we're paying attention, if we have eyes that are able to see. And we can experience God's amazing love and mercy when we look to the Cross. For as we envision God's very own Son laying down His life for us, we begin to understand how loved and forgiven we really are—we begin to experience God in a very real and personal way.

So maybe it is possible to see God. And as we see Him, we begin to know Him. And as we know Him, we begin to experience a relationship, relating to Him on a real and personal level. And we start to understand what His awesome love and incredible mercy are really all about. And then we have found Him! But that's just the beginning.

he Lord is my security

section two
don't be a fool

Fools think they need no advice,
but the wise listen to others.

Proverbs 12:15, NLT

Take Good Advice

If you want to be wise, you'll appreciate hearing good advice and you'll take that advice seriously. But a fool likes to blab on and on–like he already knows everything–and then he falls flat on his face. PROVERBS 10:8

We all act foolish sometimes, yet most of us don't want to be considered a fool all the time. But what makes a person become a fool in the first place? Surely he doesn't just wake up one morning and decide, "Hey, I guess I'll start being a fool today." Like so many other things in life, it's probably a much more gradual process. And yet the road to foolishness speeds up considerably when someone chooses to totally ignore any and all good advice. Because the fact is this: A fool assumes he already knows everything. In other words, no one can tell a fool what to do.

But if you're wise—or just want to appear wise—you'll know when to keep your mouth shut, and you'll also know how to listen to others, especially when they know more about something than you do.

Let's say you're taking a scuba class at the community pool. And there's this guy in the class who acts like he knows it all. He doesn't pay much attention to the instructor and likes to make everything into a big joke. And people in the class are pretty entertained by his antics. Then the big day finally comes when the class is ready to make its first open-water dive—out in the ocean. Who's going to want to have this guy as a diving buddy? He might've been a crack-up back at the pool, but who really wants to go fifty feet underwater and put her life in the hands of the class clown? Talk about being all wet!

So next time you're tempted to act like you know it all, remember where it can take you. And don't be too proud to take good advice. Like when you're not sure if you took the right turnoff or not, why not just stop and ask for directions? Otherwise you might end up really lost!

Keep Your Eyes Open

If you're wise you'll keep your eyes wide open, you'll watch where you're going, and you'll be prepared for what lies ahead. But a fool pretends like everything's cool and convinces himself (and anyone who'll listen) that "Hey, nothing can go wrong here." And then, wham! He gets the rug ripped out from under him. PROVERBS 14:8

How safe would you feel as the passenger in a car while the driver speeds down the freeway—with his eyes closed? Pretty dumb question, huh? But sometimes that's just the way we navigate through life. Maybe not so much in an actual physical sense, but too often we forget to open our *spiritual* eyes. Too often we plod along like zombies, barely noticing which way we're going.

God wants us to keep our spiritual eyes wide open. He wants us to learn to see and discern things with our hearts so we don't go stumbling around like fools in the dark. He knows that developing spiritual eyesight will protect us from things we can't see with our physical eyes. For instance, someone invites you to a party. It sounds pretty fun and a couple of your friends are going to be there, but deep inside you feel this gentle nudge— and it's telling you not to go. You sense that God is trying to show you something. And hopefully you pay attention and decide not to go. That's using your spiritual insight.

A fool doesn't want to use his spiritual eyes. He just blindly blunders along, often hurting himself and lots of other people along the way. Even worse, a fool pretends that danger doesn't exist, but the next thing you know he's crashed and burned.

So ask God to help you develop your spiritual vision and fine-tune your discernment. That way, not only will you know the best way to go; you'll probably avoid being caught in a head-on with a fool who's not even looking!

If you reject criticism, you only harm yourself;
but if you listen to correction,
you grow in understanding.

PROVERBS 15:32, NLT

Choose Right

A fool thinks it's cool to break rules;
he really gets a kick out of being disobedient.
But if you're wise you'll get real satisfaction, and real
pleasure, from making smart choices. PROVERBS 10:23

There's this place inside all of us that really enjoys that feeling of occasionally doing something wild and reckless. And sometimes we think that means breaking the rules. But we need to understand that God has tons of adventure and excitement in store for us—*without* breaking any rules. And the only way to get to the really good times is to choose right—and that means we choose God!

But a fool never figures this out. A fool continues right along on his reckless way—breaking the rules, cheating here, lying there—living for the moment and laughing about the chaos that follows in his wake. A fool never figures out that her careless lifestyle will never really fulfill her. And a fool can't see that he's fallen into a hopeless trap, or taken a road that leads right into a dead end.

But when we choose wisdom (by choosing God), we find real satisfaction. And as we make smart decisions, we discover that the rewards last for more than just the moment. And we realize that life is actually full of exciting risks and fun challenges—that don't involve fines or jail time! And we discover that we can derive a great deal of pleasure from doing what God wants us to do. Not only that, but we enjoy a liberating sense of freedom, not to mention the ability to sleep soundly at night. A fool misses out on so much!

Keep Your Cool

A fool can easily explode into anger. His fury is fast and hot. But if you're wise, you'll stay cool and just chill (and count to ten if necessary). PROVERBS 12:16

One of the easiest ways to spot a fool is when you see him losing his head. Well, not literally (although it's been known to happen upon occasion and isn't pretty when it does). But when you see someone who habitually explodes into anger, spewing his fury onto everyone within earshot, you can be relatively sure he's a fool. Just don't let it be you doing that!

And yet it can be hard to control your temper. Sometimes you just want to vent a little. Especially when people (like nagging parents or smart-mouthed little sisters) push all your buttons. You *want* to keep your cool, but sometimes it just feels like mission impossible. So what do you do?

Once again, it's time to go to God. Remember, He's the one who gives us wisdom; in other words, He prevents us from being fools. And if we ask Him—and mean it—He promises to give us self-control. Now, what we do with self-control is totally up to us. But if we really want to be wise, we'll begin to put it into use—we'll practice using it. And hopefully we'll discover some practical ways to control ourselves, like slowly counting to ten—or even a hundred, if necessary! Or maybe we'll learn to take a deep breath and simply walk away from a volatile situation, waiting until we cool off before we deal with it.

But here's the really great thing about keeping your cool: You feel really good afterward when you realize the temper trap you just avoided. And that's really cool!

Those who are short-tempered do foolish things.

don't hang with a fool

Stay away from fools,

for you won't find knowledge there.

Proverbs 14:7, NLT

Trusting oneself
is foolish, but
those who walk in
wisdom are safe.

Fools Won't Fess Up

Even when a fool blows it, he won't admit it to anyone, and he's never sorry. But don't be like that. Admit your mistakes, and then ask God to forgive you. PROVERBS 14:9

Okay, we all mess up sometimes. It's just part of being human. But the difference between a fool and one who's not a fool is that the fool will never fess up to his mistakes. The fool goes around acting like he did absolutely nothing wrong—and if you're his buddy, he'll try to convince you to do the same. You see, a fool *never* takes responsibility for his own actions—it's always "someone else's fault."

And even though it's hard to admit when you've blown it (especially if you've blown it more than once), the alternative can be pretty scary—not to mention humiliating. Because the more we try to hide or bury our mistakes, the bigger and uglier they become. It's kind of like having a huge zit on your nose that you try to disguise beneath a glob of white Clearasil, which only makes it stand out more. And to make matters worse, the zit just keeps on growing and growing, threatening to erupt like Mount St. Helens.

And besides, even if we somehow *do* manage to conceal our blunders for a little while, God can still see them. And before long others can too. It's always better to just step forward and come clean.

First you need to admit to yourself that you blew it. Then you need to admit your mistake to God and ask Him to forgive you. And you might even need to admit this blunder to others (especially if your faux pas has hurt them too). Then, when it's all said and done, don't forget to forgive yourself. Because if God can forgive you, who are you to hold back?

Fools Love Gossip

A fool loves to tell other people's secrets—even when her facts aren't exactly accurate. You can never totally trust a chick who gossips. And don't hang out with a guy who's constantly talking about others. PROVERBS 20:19

Most people won't admit it, but everyone enjoys a juicy bit of gossip from time to time—or at least they think they do. But like a bad piece of meat, which tasted pretty good going down, gossip can make you feel pretty sick later. But a fool just loves to gossip—and the more sensational the story, the better she likes it. In fact, a fool will even twist the facts to make his tale more exciting and entertaining. And he thinks nothing of destroying someone's reputation for his own enjoyment (or to make himself look better).

But God wants us to stay away from fools like that. And He wants us to be smart enough to know that gossip is seriously harmful—whether we're actually passing it along or simply standing around listening.

So the next time you get caught in a gossip circle, remember that you have several options: 1) You can attempt to change the subject; 2) you can defend the person who's getting smeared; or 3) you can just walk away. And don't forget to take a moment to pray and invite God to direct you in this. Because who knows what might happen? For example, the "fool" repeating the gossip might not be a true fool after all, and she might actually appreciate someone who cares enough to set her straight. Or she could get totally ticked at you. But don't feel too bad; that's just the natural reaction of someone who truly is a fool. And don't forget to pray for her. Because even though she's a fool, God can still rescue her from herself.

Fire goes out for lack of fuel, and quarrels disappear when gossip stops.

PROVERBS 26:20, NLT

Don't Follow a Fool

Don't follow a fool—anywhere. And don't hang out on his turf; surely you can find someplace better to go. Because a fool will not rest until he stirs up some kind of trouble or really trips somebody up. PROVERBS 4:14-16

For some reason, fools often want to be leaders. And that's when they're on the lookout for someone who will just blindly follow them. It's probably because it makes them feel like they're actually heading in the right direction, when in reality they're destined for a lonely stay at Heartbreak Hotel. But remember, it's just another classic characteristic of fools—*they're fooling themselves.* Just don't let them take you along for the ride.

So how do you avoid getting taken in by fools? How do you keep them from leading you somewhere you know you shouldn't go—like a drinking party or something you know is off-limits? It's simple. First of all, don't put yourself into a close friendship with fools. And next, don't hang out where they hang out, because where fools gather, trouble usually lurks.

But here's the tricky part: We know that God wants us to love everyone—*including fools.* And it stands to reason that He wants to use us to show His love for them. He just doesn't want us to get tangled up with them in the process. So once again, we have to keep our spiritual eyes wide open. And we need to pray

specifically that God will give us the wisdom to know the difference between helping someone and being pulled into their
foolish and dangerous schemes.

Here's the good news: This all becomes much easier with
practice and over time. And instead of being led by a fool, you
may actually end up leading him. That is, unless you're dealing
with a real die-hard fool. But even then, you can still pray—
because, as we all know, nothing's too difficult for God. And
only God can save a fool.

Fools Love to Argue

**When fools want to argue (like they so often do), don't let
yourself get sucked into the debate, or you might become as
foolish as they are.** PROVERBS 26:4

Have you ever noticed how much fools like to argue? Just
get caught in the cross fire and you'll soon realize how
much they love to engage in verbal warfare. And you'll see how
they try to suck you right in too. But watch out, because that's
when they'll really let you have it—right smack between the eyes!

Why is that? Well, it's yet another classic characteristic of
fools—they're just trying to *fool themselves*. They want to believe
that they're really right. And if they can argue long enough,
loud enough, or fervently enough—well, maybe then they'll

convince themselves. And if they get lucky, maybe they'll convince someone else along the way too.

But remember this: Just because a fool "wins" an argument, it doesn't necessarily make her right—even though a real fool believes that winning validates her opinion (and remember, that's why she gets in an argument in the first place). Usually it's just better not to get involved. Because even if you do manage to make some valid points, they usually get trampled in the mucky mess of the debate anyway. Besides that, a fool loves to twist and manipulate the truth and make it look like it's a lie. So most of the time you're wise to just step back and express to that person that arguing accomplishes nothing. In other words, agree to disagree.

If you really believe that God is telling you to pursue this debate, then proceed with caution and don't forget to pray along the way. Because who knows, maybe this person isn't a real fool after all. And maybe God will use your influence to make a difference. And if not, you can still pray that your words will be like seeds that can sprout later. Even a fool can be rescued when the timing's right.

Don't waste your breath on fools, for they will despise the wisest advice.

section four
watch your words

A gentle answer turns away wrath,
but harsh words stir up anger.

Proverbs 15:1, NLT

A Good Word

When God leads, you're able to give good advice.... And the words you speak will be encouraging and helpful. PROVERBS 10:31-32

Words have such power. They can wound or heal, build up or tear down. And yet we take our words for granted. We lightly toss them out, barely considering what kind of impact they might have at the time, or even later on down the line. "They're just words," you might say, or "Talk is cheap." But if you really considered the effect your words can have, you would probably use them a lot more carefully.

For instance, what's worth more than some really sound advice? Say you're trying to decide which college to apply to and a trustworthy friend tells you about a fantastic scholarship program at a really good school. How much are those words worth to you? But good advice doesn't always have a monetary tag attached to it. Sometimes it's just a good friend who sets you straight and helps you avoid making a painful mistake. And all this is achieved with mere words. Pretty powerful stuff!

And you have that same power too—right on the tip of your tongue. You can help and encourage others with your words. Every single day you interact with all sorts of people, and in each situation your words have the power to make a big difference in someone's life—for better or for worse. But to have a *really* positive influence requires a little forethought and planning, not to mention self-control (like when you're tempted to say something sarcastic or just plain lame). But most of all it takes a heart that's tuned in to God. Because He's the one who can give us just the right words. And those words can make all the difference.

Telling the Truth

When you live an honest life, you will stay out of harm's way. But those who cheat and lie fall into ruin. PROVERBS 28:18

We've all heard that "Honesty is the best policy," but do we really believe it? And do we live it out on a daily basis? Or do we occasionally feel tempted to just tweak the truth a little? Like maybe you stretch the truth to make yourself look slightly better to someone else. Or perhaps you exaggerate an accomplishment to impress a friend. Or maybe you're not quite honest when you think stretching the truth might protect you from an uncomfortable consequence.

Like say you slipped in thirty minutes past your curfew last night, but your parents were sound asleep, snoring like a couple of grizzly bears. So when they ask you about it this morning, you just say, "Hey, no problem. I was in on time." And maybe you think that it's just a little white lie, and besides, what they don't know won't hurt them. But be honest, wouldn't they feel hurt if they knew you had lied to them?

Of course, there are some really good and practical reasons why it's not smart to lie (things like getting caught and looking stupid). But there are some even more important spiritual reasons as well. Because the fact is that when we're dishonest, it not only hurts others (when they find us out), but it also hurts us by creating a barrier between God and us. And if we continue to lie without admitting it and asking God to forgive us, that barrier will just grow and grow. And pretty soon our relationship with God will really suffer. And then we'll be seriously hurting. So why not keep your life simple and just stick to the truth!

Weigh Your Words

Don't talk too much or you may say something really stupid, something that's wrong and hurts someone else. Get smart and realize when you've said enough. PROVERBS 10:19

Have you ever noticed how the more you talk and joke around, the more superficial and sarcastic the conversation can become? Not everyone has this problem, of course, but it's fairly common and can really take a toll on friendships. It's like you're just hanging out with your buddies, and you're all relaxed, gabbing and sharing a few laughs. But if you're too careless, it's easy to say something you'll be sorry for later. And it's really tough to take back your words.

But maybe as we learn to value our words more, we'll realize that we don't need to just blurt out every single thought that crosses our mind. It's possible to learn how to sift our words *before* we speak, and we can avoid those words that might get misconstrued or hurt someone.

Naturally this is a skill that takes time and practice, and some folks never do figure it out. But if you really want to learn how to avoid "foot-in-mouth" disease, you'll ask God to increase your self-discipline and teach you how to control your tongue. You'll begin to understand that keeping your mouth shut really isn't that painful after all. And it's amazing how much better the mind works when the lips are silent for a few moments!

Another little side benefit: You'll become a better listener too and, consequently, a better friend. And what could be better than that?

If you keep your mouth shut, you will stay out of trouble.

PROVERBS 21:23, NLT

Keep It Clean

Don't swear or cuss. And avoid situations that tempt you to use coarse language. PROVERBS 4:24

Some people wonder what all the fuss is about. Like what's really wrong with using a four-letter word now and then? I mean, just go to a movie or a sporting event or even walk down the hall at school and you're sure to hear plenty of words that might curl your grandmother's hair. But isn't it just part of our culture these days? Does anyone really care? They're just words, after all.

But if you stop and really think about the meaning of the words—the real meaning—you might begin to hear things differently. And if you stopped and asked yourself, "Am I truly honoring God with my speech?" you might want to begin speaking differently too. For instance, why would you want to use God's name or Jesus' name to vent or to express your anger? It just doesn't make sense, does it? Sure, maybe if you were really praying to Him, but if you're just saying "Jesus Christ!" as a release for your frustration, then you need to reexamine your relationship with Him.

The good thing is that God can show you what's right for you—if you ask Him, that is. Because God cares about you and wants to redirect your speech so that it's pleasing to Him. You just need to be willing to listen to that quiet voice inside you

Fools spout only foolishness

and then put those wise words into practice. And before long, you'll discover that your tongue is a lot like the rudder used to steer a big ship: Once you've got it under control, you can sail right through the roughest seas with no problem!

The mouths of fools are their ruin; their lips get them into trouble.

section five
wisdom hunt

Cry out for insight and understanding.
    Search for them as you would for lost money
or hidden treasure.

Proverbs 2:3–4, NLT

Beginning of Wisdom

When we respect and honor God, wholeheartedly believing
that He alone is God, then we'll begin to experience
real wisdom. And as we get to know God personally and
intimately, we'll grow even wiser, and our understanding will
deepen. PROVERBS 9:10

Real wisdom begins and ends with God, and He's the only
one who can really dispense it. So if we're honestly looking for real wisdom, we'd better start looking at God. And for-
tunately for us, He's ready to share His wisdom. He just wants
us to come to Him and ask. Sounds pretty simple, doesn't it?
Then what keeps us from doing it? What's holding us back? Are
we worried that we'll turn into geeks or nerds if we suddenly
become too wise? Or could it be that we don't really understand what wisdom is all about?

The reason we don't totally understand wisdom is probably
because we don't totally understand God (since in essence He *is*
wisdom). But if we take time to get to know God better—on a
personal level—we can't help but become wiser in the process.
And as we know God better, our love and respect for Him
grow, which in turn makes us even wiser. It's like He rubs off
on us.

Say you make a new friend who plays ball like Michael
Jordan. You hang out with him a lot, and for fun you shoot

Learn to be wise, and develop good judgment.

hoops down at the park. Before long, your game really starts to improve. Maybe you don't even notice it's happening, but it is. You see, it's just the natural result of hanging with your new friend.

And it's no different with God. The more time we spend with Him, the wiser we'll be. And that wisdom can guide us through a life that's more exciting and fulfilling than anything we've ever dreamed of!

Wisdom Protects You

When you know God and your heart's full of His wisdom, you will be filled with joy, because God helps you make wise choices—choices that keep you safe. For wisdom is like a giant shield that protects you. PROVERBS 2:10-11

We live in a dangerous world. And without God it can be pretty scary too. But when we really know God and have His wisdom in us, we have nothing to fear. But, of course, it doesn't always feel that way. Sometimes we forget that God's watching out for us, or that He's ready to give us the wisdom we need so we can face the challenges of the day. And that's when we start freaking out—and suddenly it can feel like everyone's out to get us!

But if we can just pause long enough to remember *who* God

is, and *what* He wants to do in our lives, wisdom will return to us, and with it will come a deep sense of peace.

Let's say that wisdom is like this fantastic Beverly Hills mansion that we get to live in—for free! It's fully equipped with everything from a well-stocked kitchen to a big-screen surround-sound TV with a DVD player. It even has a swimming pool and a bowling alley! It has absolutely everything we could ever want or need. On top of everything else, it's got this state-of-the-art security system that keeps us totally safe. Now why would we ever want to leave that kind of life?

But sometimes we just walk right out the front door and past the tall security gates, and as a result we get hit with all kinds of trouble and heartache and pain. You see, that's what happens when we walk away from wisdom. It's like we step outside of God's provision and protection. But the good news is that *He always welcomes us back.* And the more we understand who God is, the less we want to walk away.

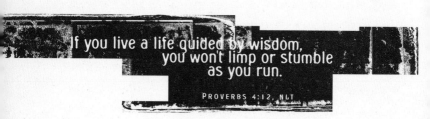

If you live a life guided by wisdom,
you won't limp or stumble
as you run.

PROVERBS 4:12, NLT

Wisdom's Worth

What you can gain from wisdom is worth more than all the money on Wall Street, and the final payoff is tons more valuable than all the gold in Fort Knox. Wisdom is more precious than rubies and diamonds, and nothing you can ever desire will ever compare with wisdom. PROVERBS 3:14-15

Remember the old "What would you do if you could have one wish granted?" question? If you were smart you'd say, "I wish for three more wishes." Then you could wish for lots of stuff, including more wishes. Thousands of years ago there was a man who was asked a similar question. God asked King Solomon what he most wanted, and Solomon said he wanted to rule His people with wisdom. God was so pleased with Solomon's answer that He granted him his wish, and Solomon is said to have been the wisest man in all of history (1 Kings 3).

But here's the irony: Solomon wasn't just the wisest man on earth; he was the richest one too. As a result of utilizing his wisdom, Solomon's kingdom and wealth far exceeded anything anyone had ever seen. But that's how it is with wisdom: When you really have it, everything else just seems to follow. Whether it's wealth or success or health or happiness—anything worthwhile seems to be directly connected to wisdom.

Does that mean you'll automatically get rich if you become wise? Maybe. But more important, you'll begin to understand that there are various sorts of "riches." And you'll appreciate that having real wisdom is worth a lot more than all the money in the world. And you won't want to trade it for anything. You'll realize that real wisdom comes only from knowing God, and it's worth hanging on to.

Wisdom is far more valuable than rubies. Nothing you desire can be compared with it.

section six
the good life

> True humility and fear of the LORD
> lead to riches, honor, and long life.
>
> *Proverbs 22:4, NLT*

The way of the righteous is like the first gleam of dawn.

A Good Reputation

Always remember what God has taught you so that you'll live long and have a totally cool life. Be loyal and kind to those around you, but don't fake it—do it from your heart. Because that's what pleases God (and others too). And then you'll have a good name. PROVERBS 3:1-4

Do you care what other people think of you? Maybe you try not to think about it too much because maybe it seems shallow and superficial to worry about how others perceive you. But be honest now, does your image—the way people see you—really matter? The Bible talks quite a bit about having a "good name," which is the same as having a good image or a good reputation (the way people think about you). And how do you get a good name anyway?

The best way to achieve a good name is simply to live well. And that means living the way God has shown you is best—*for you.* That basically means listening to and obeying God. Now, sometimes it might seem hard to obey God all the time. But when you do, the payoffs are huge—and lasting.

And in time, others start to notice too. They can see that something is very different about your life. They may see how you're loyal to your friends and kind to the people around you. And they can tell you're not faking it either—you're not a hypocrite. And that means a lot.

As your reputation grows, people begin to trust you more. They come to you with questions; they might even ask you for help. It's definitely a very good place to be. But remember, only God can get you there.

Good Plans

Stay focused on good planning, because it's the key to a really fantastic life—a life that is honored and respected by others.

PROVERBS 3:21-22

Maybe you've heard the saying "Fail to plan, plan to fail." Well, we can't plan every single minute of our lives (since God has His own plans for us), but we can probably plan a little better than we usually do. And the best way to achieve a successful plan is to bring all our plans before God, and then ask Him to direct them—and to bless them. And when we do this one thing, it's amazing how the pressure is alleviated. Because suddenly we can relax; we can trust God to get us wherever it is we need to go.

Can you imagine what it would be like to sail a boat across the Pacific without some prior planning? Or to fly through space in a shuttle without any previous preparations? Any challenging journey starts out with weeks, months, sometimes even years of careful and strategic planning in order to succeed.

So why would you think your life is any different? Whether you realize it or not, you're making small (and large) choices every single day—choices that play right into your life's plan. When you choose wisely and listen to God's quiet voice, you lay the foundations for a really great life. But when you consistently make stupid choices (that perhaps feel good at the moment), you're preparing yourself for real disappointment and a totally unfulfilling life. So why not start asking God about His plans for you?

Good Health

Don't start thinking you're so great and smart! Instead, focus on God's power and wisdom and love, and then do what's right. As a result you'll have good health and energy that will see you through. PROVERBS 3:7-8

When we're young, it's easy to take our health for granted. We think we can do anything—climb any mountain, surf any wave. It's almost as if we think we're indestructible. That is, until we get sick or take a tumble and break something important like an arm or a leg. Then we might start respecting something as seemingly simple as good health.

But even if you haven't had your health threatened, it's not too early to begin understanding the way it works. For instance, do you realize how much your spiritual health impacts your physical health? And did you know that your spiritual health is a direct result of your relationship with God?

It's like God is our true energy source, and as long as we're connected with Him, we can function at our peak level. Imagine a CD player (with rechargeable batteries): You plug it into the wall, and it can play music forever. When it's unplugged, it can still go for a few hours, but it'll slowly run out of juice and the music will start to sound sluggish and finally stop altogether. But just plug that baby back into the power source and you're in business again.

And that's how it is with us. Our hearts are happier and we have more energy and life when we're plugged into God—our power source! It's the ultimate way to stay healthy. And the good thing about God is that He never has an energy crisis. He can keep us up and running forever!

A cheerful heart is good medicine.

PROVERBS 17:22, NLT

good friends

Never abandon a friend—
        either yours or your father's.

Proverbs 27:10, NLT

The godly give good advice to their friends.

Good Advice

Even your coolest plans can fall to pieces when you forget to ask others for advice. But when you ask those who love you for their honest opinions, you're sure to succeed.

PROVERBS 15:22

It's great to have lots of friends. And it can be fun to just hang out, or joke around, or just do nothing in general. But when you really need someone to talk to, who do you call? Don't you usually call your *best* friend? Isn't that what makes best friends anyway—the fact that they're always there for you? And when you really need some good and honest advice, don't you usually go to your best friend to get it?

That's why it's so important to have a really good friend. You need someone you can trust with your problems, someone who really cares about you, someone who won't betray you. That way you'll know that they're really telling it to you straight.

But sometimes it's hard to know the difference between a really good friend and a not-so-good friend. Or when someone who seems totally cool comes along and wants to be your new friend, and suddenly you feel confused. Maybe you're even tempted to just push an old friend aside. And then what kind of friend does that make you?

Of course, there are no easy answers to these questions. But if you ask God, He can lead you—He can show you the friends who are best for you. You just have to be honest and willing to listen. And then you need to make sure you're becoming the kind of friend you'd like to have. Because the truth is life's always a lot easier with a good friend by your side.

Good Company

Even if all you have to eat is a measly bowl of pork 'n' beans, it always tastes better when you eat it with a good friend. But the finest T-bone steak can be as tasteless as a Milk-Bone when you eat it with someone who hates you. PROVERBS 15:17

It's amazing how little it takes to have a good time when you're with someone you really like. A bike ride becomes a wild adventure. An ice cream cone becomes a gourmet treat. Just because you're with a good friend.

And that's just the way God wants it to be. He knows how much we need each other. And He knows that we enjoy life a whole lot more when we've got someone to share it with. That's what good friends are for.

Many will say they are loyal friends, but who can find one who is really faithful?

PROVERBS 20:6, NLT

But occasionally we can be distracted by a friend who offers lots of *action* but not much *satisfaction*. Maybe this type of "friend" comes up with all kinds of crazy ideas and activities, but when the day is over, you realize that it really wasn't that much fun. And maybe it's because that person really isn't that good of a friend in the first place. Maybe you know he's not the kind of guy that would stick with you when things got tough. Or maybe it's because you finally understand that in the long run the "coolest" friend isn't necessarily the *best* kind of friend. So why not ask God to show you how to recognize who your true friends really are, and then commit yourself to be equally true to them.

Good Influence

When you hang with friends who are sensible and have their heads on straight, you'll have a good time and avoid trouble. But if you hang with jerks, you better expect to be jerked around. PROVERBS 13:20

Admit it, you would never pick a friend just because you thought he or she might be a "good influence" on you. That's like something your parents would want you to do! But whether you can admit it or not, your friends *do* influence you. And in the same way, you influence them. Like it or not, it happens. It's just the result of two people hanging together. Before long, they start to act alike, they listen to the same music, and they even dress similarly. If you don't think it's true, just look at various groups of friends and you'll see.

So if you can admit that friends might actually influence each other, can you also see how your friends might be influencing you? Is it for good? Or not?

Do your friends know God? Or do they make fun of Him? Are they trying to live their lives for God? Or are they living each day for themselves? Do they encourage you to do what's right, even when it's not the easiest thing to do? Or do they nudge you to step over the line now and then? Really think about it: Do your friends really, truly have your best interests in mind? Or do they dare you to take unnecessary risks; do they urge you to do what you know is wrong?

And if you're fortunate enough to have good friends who really care about you, have you considered what kind of influence you are on them? Have you asked God to help you become a loyal and dependable friend to them, the kind of friend that God wants to be to you?

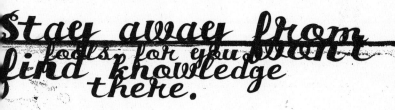

stay away from fools, for you won't find knowledge there.

section eight
family stuff

Listen to your father, who gave you life,
and don't despise your mother's experience when she is old.
Get the truth and don't ever sell it;
also get wisdom, discipline, and discernment.

Proverbs 23:22—23, NLT

Listen to Your Parents

Don't tune out your dad, but listen carefully, especially when he's trying to tell you something important. And don't ignore your mom, but pay close attention when she's trying to explain something. Your parents can still teach you a thing or two, and life will go a lot easier and be a whole lot better if you really listen to them. PROVERBS 1:8-9

Okay, it's not always easy to listen to your parents. And yeah, they're not always right about absolutely everything. But even so, you need to remember that God's the one who chose them to parent you, and when you don't respect them it's like you're not respecting God. So even when you don't feel like it or it seems like they're nagging, you still need to try to listen better.

But as you probably know by now, there's more to listening than just hearing the words. And we've all been guilty of tunnel brain syndrome—words going in one ear and rapidly exiting the other. But as you grow older and hopefully wiser, you should start to appreciate that your parents really have learned a thing or two during their lifetime. And believe it or not, they were once the exact same age as you are right now, and they probably went through some very similar struggles.

So don't be so worried about opening up to your parents with your problems. Chances are they already suspect that life isn't going perfectly smoothly for you anyway (remember, they were teenagers once). And they just might have a word of advice that could prove really practical to your situation. Besides that, God can speak to you through them, and it can really pay off to listen and then actually *take* their advice.

Accept Discipline

If you want to become mature and capable and competent to deal with life's challenges, you'll need to learn not only to accept but even to love discipline. It's totally senseless to get upset when you're corrected. And it's incredibly stupid to hate being disciplined. PROVERBS 12:1

Who likes to be caught in the wrong? I mean it's bad enough to make a stupid mistake, but it feels even worse when someone shines the spotlight on you and points out your blunder in front of everyone. It's humiliating. And our natural human reaction is to try to minimize the problem, like, "Hey, it's no big deal." Or maybe we even try to act like we didn't do it in the first place, or that it wasn't really our fault. It's uncomfortable when someone points a finger at us or tries to correct us. It makes us feel dumb and immature.

But that's not how God wants us to view discipline and correction. He wants us to grow up enough that we can start to realize that, whether or not it feels good, it's really good for us. And besides that, life will go much more smoothly for us when we learn to actually welcome discipline.

Let's say you accidentally run a stop sign and a cop happens to be parked right around the corner. He flips on his flashing lights and pulls you over and tells you that you blew it. How's he going to react if you get all mad at him, or deny the offense, or act like it's someone else's fault? Do you think it'll make him lighten up on you? Ha—think again! Of course you probably already figured this out by now, but your best response is to simply come clean, admit you blew it, apologize, and then listen respectfully to his little safety lecture. And who knows, maybe you'll get off with just a warning this time. (Just don't think it'll work if you run that stop sign again.)

So grow up and learn to accept and even appreciate it when someone (especially a parent) is trying to straighten you out. Because you know deep down that it's really for your own good and it's because your parents love you.

It is painful to be the parent of a fool; there is no joy for the father of a rebel.

PROVERBS 17:21, NLT

Happy Parents

The parents of kids who love God have good reason to be totally happy. Because it's pure joy to have kids who are becoming wise! So go ahead and make your parents really happy; show them that their hard work is starting to pay off. PROVERBS 23:24-25

You probably don't spend a whole lot of time just thinking up ways to make your parents happy. In fact, if you're like most kids, you're probably more concerned with the many ways your parents could make *your* life happier. But as we get older and appreciate our parents more, we might start thinking of how we can make life a little better for them. Because it's not easy being a parent, and most of the time it's a pretty thankless job.

But when you're really walking with God and trying to live your life to please Him, whether they know it or not, your parents will really benefit from your good choices. And when you're doing well, your parents are a whole lot happier. And who doesn't want happier parents? Of course, you're not living your life just to make your parents happy. But it's a nice little perk for doing what's right.

Besides, isn't there enough pain and trouble in this world? Sometimes a little happiness can carry a stressed-out parent a long way. Not to mention the way it can improve the environment at home. So why not give your parents some real pleasure and let them know that you're really trying to stay connected to God. And then notice how the choices you're making really do bring your parents a deep sense of relief and joy. Sure, they might not be jumping up and down, but if you look closely, you'll probably see it in their eyes. And for sure, God will be smiling on you!

Sensible children bring joy to their father.

section nine

a handle on money

Trust in your money and down you go!

    But the godly flourish like leaves in spring.

Proverbs 11:28, NLT

Hard Work Pays Off

Lazy folks might want everything they see and then end up with absolutely nothing. But when you do your best and work hard, you not only get ahead in this world, but you feel good about yourself too. PROVERBS 13:4

No one really likes to be called "lazy," and yet to be perfectly honest, you have to admit that we do enjoy our leisure time. And there's nothing wrong with a little R and R—we all need some down time occasionally. But too much kicking back can mess you up if you're not careful. And interestingly enough, the book of Proverbs has more verses about laziness than almost any other subject.

In other words, God is probably trying to warn us against the dangers of being unmotivated (or lazy). Is it because He's worried that there's work to be done and no one will do it if we just sit around on our hind ends in front of the TV all day? Or is it because He understands how we need to be involved and engaged in order to live truly fulfilled lives?

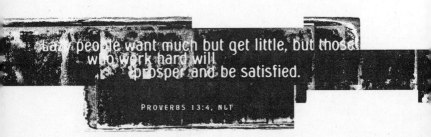

Lazy people want much but get little, but those who work hard will prosper and be satisfied.

PROVERBS 13:4, NLT

You see, God has designed us with minds and hands that need to be kept busy. The truth is that *when we do nothing, we become nothing*. But when we put our energies into something (whether it's school or work or volunteering or whatever), we become more complete and fulfilled. And we feel a lot better about ourselves at the end of the day.

So don't be afraid to roll up your sleeves and work hard, even if the task seems trivial or meaningless or too hard, because you can count on the fact that God has His eye on you. And He'll reward you for giving it your best effort. And someday, whether in this world or the next, your investment will have a really great payoff.

Be Generous

God loves to see you give generously, sharing what you have with those who have less. And He'll reward and bless you for your kindness. PROVERBS 22:9

If you're worried that you won't have what you need when you need it, it's easy to become a tightwad. Maybe you worry that your money and resources will suddenly disappear—and then where will you be? But can you see that you're not trusting God to take care of you? And when you don't trust God, you're not only anxious, but stingy as well. Because how can you possibly share anything with someone else when you're always afraid you're going to run out for yourself?

But if we really believe that God's the one who gives us what we need, it's not hard to be generous. We start to understand how everything we own has come from God, and as a result we don't cling to our material possessions so much. We begin to realize that our money is really God's money and that He has plenty to go around (after all, He owns the whole world!). And suddenly it's easier to share with those who are in need.

Not only is it easier, but we also discover how giving to others brings real joy and fulfillment to us. That verse really is true—it really is better to give than to receive!

And before we know it, we've set an amazing cycle into motion. We're trusting God to take care of us, and as a result we're sharing what we have with others. And because God is pleased with our generosity, He's blessing us with even more! And what could be better than that?

A greedy person tries to get rich quick, but it only leads to poverty.

PROVERBS 28:22, NLT

True Riches

It's a lot better to be a really good person than to be filthy rich. Having a good reputation and the respect of others is worth more than a billion dollars. PROVERBS 22:1

Which would you rather have: a billion dollars or a good name? Now for clarification, a good name isn't like Julia Roberts or Magic Johnson (although those are nice enough names). A truly good name (like we've talked about before) means having an excellent reputation as well as the respect of your peers. So be honest, which is more appealing—name or wealth? Okay, maybe you're thinking if you had all that money you could just go out and buy yourself a good name.

Nice try, but the truth is that a good name can't be bought, not with any amount of money. Just look at some of the richest people in the world who came by their wealth wrongly, and you'll see that they're not respected. A good name can only be earned. And the only way you earn a good name is by the way you live. And that means living the way God has called you to live.

And when you live your life God's way, you can't help but receive all kinds of blessings—and you might even acquire some material wealth as well. Or maybe not. But more importantly, you'll have the kind of life that money can't buy. You'll have those priceless treasures like joy and peace and love and happiness.

Honor the Lord with your wealth

And here's the coolest part: When you choose a good name over wealth, the day will come when you'll stand before God and He'll actually *know your name!* Now if you'd chosen riches instead, He might not even know you. Then where would you be? So go for the sure thing—go with the name!

A wise youth works hard...a youth who sleeps away the hour of opportunity brings shame.

guard your heart

Above all else,

guard your heart,

for it affects everything you do.

Proverbs 4:23, NLT

Abstain from Sex

Why would you go around just casually having sex with anyone who came along? Why not save this once-in-a-lifetime event (the first time) for the right one? Why not share this very special relationship with the one you marry? Don't waste this precious gift on mere acquaintances. PROVERBS 5:16-17

Despite our culture's general acceptance of sex both prior to and outside of marriage, God makes it perfectly clear that it's unacceptable. But He doesn't "just say no" to sex because He's an old curmudgeon who doesn't want anyone to have any fun. He says no because He knows what's in our best interest. He understands that when we engage in a sexual relationship, it's more than just a "physical thing." Because whether we can admit it to ourselves or not, our hearts become involved, and we ultimately get hurt. Sometimes we get hurt so badly that we carry the wounds and scars with us for the rest of our lives. And God loves us too much to encourage that.

The pleasure of having sex with someone you love is a beautiful gift—something to be treasured. And God wants us to wait and experience that gift with the one we commit to in marriage—the one we will spend the rest of our lives with.

Do you remember being a kid at Christmastime? You were staring in fascination at a brightly wrapped package beneath the Christmas tree. It had your name on it and you had no idea what it might contain. Then when your parents weren't around, you sneaked the package off into a closet and carefully slit open the paper with a sharp knife and unwrapped the present to discover that it was just what you'd wanted. Then, worried your parents would soon be back, you quickly rewrapped the gift and returned it to its place under the tree. But how did you feel when Christmas came and you opened the present and the surprise was spoiled?

In a way, that's what it's like when we choose to disobey God and have sex before marriage. We spoil the gift He has waiting for us. But the good news is that He'll forgive us, and if we ask Him, He can begin to heal the emotional and spiritual wounds we've incurred by disobeying. But why not avoid these problems and choose God's best instead?

For God knows all hearts...
And he will judge all people according
to what they have done.

PROVERBS 24:12, NLT

Control Lustful Thoughts

God's Word can keep you safe and protect you from falling into sexual temptation. But you must choose not to entertain lustful thoughts, no matter how tempting it might seem. Don't be seduced by what will ultimately hurt you. PROVERBS 6:24-26

Even when we've made the commitment to abstain from sex before marriage, it can still be a struggle to control our minds. For instance, we see certain images in movies, TV, music videos, or even at school, and we start to imagine scenarios that lead our thoughts down the wrong road. But God promises us help in this area, especially if we read (and memorize) His Word and refocus our thoughts on Him.

But we're the only ones who can make these choices. God gave us the freedom to think and decide for ourselves, and He doesn't force His will on us. Yet even when we want to choose what's right, it can still be pretty challenging at times. But then that's what life's all about, isn't it? Making choices, every day. And the more we get in the habit of making good choices—choices that honor God—the easier it gets.

And God is always ready to help. We just need to ask. He wants to lead and guide us along so we don't get caught in situations that tempt us to go the wrong way. He wants to show us what's good for us in the way of music, clothing, movies—and everything—but we've got to be willing to listen to Him. And then we've got to be willing to obey.

But the reward for obeying is huge! It starts with things like having a clear conscience and some really good relationships with both guys and girls. And then it goes on into your future as well, preparing you for a lasting and intimate relationship with the special person God has already chosen just for you. And that's totally worth waiting for!

People may be pure in their own eyes, but the Lord examines their motives.

About Marriage

Wait and let your spouse be the one who fills your life and your heart with blessings! Share immense joy and love with the one you marry! Have eyes only for your spouse, and always be satisfied and captivated by the love you find in your marriage. PROVERBS 5:18-19

You may tell people that you're too young to be thinking about marriage, but the truth is that you probably do think about it from time to time anyway. Everyone does. It's just normal. Maybe you try to imagine the person you might spend the rest of your life with. Or what it might feel like to love someone that much. And what it would feel like to have that person love you for better or for worse? And, hey, will sex be fun? And will you have kids? Most likely, all those questions, and probably lots more, have passed through your mind occasionally.

It's good to consider these things and to develop some healthy ideas about marriage in general. In a way, it's a sort of preparation. And you can actually learn a lot about marriage by reading God's Word. You can find out what makes a good marriage and what doesn't.

But then it's best to just give the whole thing back to God—to put the issue of whether or not you'll marry, or when, or to whom—back into His hands, back where it belongs. And then you can just focus on the challenges of the day—and that should be enough to keep you occupied. And believe it or not, all the friendships and relationships you're dealing with right now will in some way help prepare you for a really great marriage relationship later on.

So just as you're trusting God with your life, you'll also want to trust Him with your future and with the whole issue of marriage. And you can rest assured that God really does have your best interests in mind. And when the timing for marriage is right, you'll most likely be the first (or maybe the second) one to know!

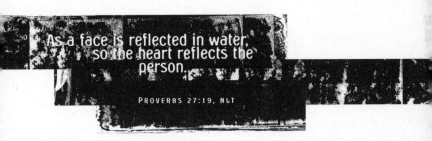

As a face is reflected in water, so the heart reflects the person.

PROVERBS 27:19, NLT

section eleven
keep the faith

"I love all who love me.
Those who search for me
will surely find me."

Proverbs 8:17, NLT

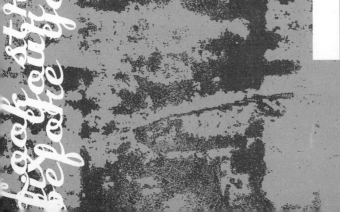

God Will Lead You

Trust God with all that you are, and don't rely on yourself for all the answers. Look for God's will in everything you do, and He'll show you the right path to take. PROVERBS 3:5-6

Does it boggle your mind a little to think that the almighty God of the universe actually wants to take the time to show you the right direction for your life? Well, if it does overwhelm you, you're not alone. But keep in mind that the only reason we struggle with accepting this fact is because we mistakenly assume that God is much, much smaller than He really is. The truth is: None of us earthlings can begin to imagine how totally huge and awesome and mighty God really is. And because of our limited thinking, we sometimes try to limit God too.

But when we limit God, we limit our faith. So instead of simply assuming that God is too small or too busy or too whatever, we need to spend time reading His Word, talking with Him, and trying to better understand His will for us. And as a result, our faith will naturally (or supernaturally) increase. And instead of just relying on our extremely limited knowledge, we'll begin to trust Him more. We'll begin to relax a little, and before long we'll just let Him lead us to wherever it is we need to go. And what a great place that is to be.

So next time you're questioning God's ability to lead you, you better stop and question your own ability to believe Him—

to trust Him and take Him at His word. Take a moment to con-
fess your doubts and invite Him to increase your faith—then let
go and let God!

As You Grow

**Keep listening to Me. For I have amazing things to tell you.
And every single thing I say is true. My advice is healthy
and good for you. And My words are simple for you to
understand.** PROVERBS 8:6, 8-9

In the same way you've grown physically and mentally over the
years, you're also growing spiritually. But the problem with
spiritual growth is that it's very hard to measure. And just when
you think you can actually see some growth, it usually backfires
and you feel even smaller than you felt before. But that's a good
thing. You see, the closer you get to God, the more flaws and
faults you can see in yourself. Does that mean you're getting
worse? Not at all! It just means you're becoming more sensitive
to what God's doing in your life.

Write [my teachings] deep
within your heart.

PROVERBS 7:3, NLT

But the real secret to spiritual growth can be found in a tree. Okay, now you're probably scratching your head and asking, "What's up with that?" Just imagine for a moment a tree—except God is the trunk of the tree and you are one of the branches. Now if you're a smart branch, you'll know that the except way to grow bigger (not to mention growing things like leaves and fruit) is to remain tightly connected to the trunk so that the life-giving sap can flow right into you.

And it's no different between us and God. We have to stay tightly connected to Him, not just so we can grow, but also to stay alive. Because how long can a branch live once it breaks away from the tree and falls to the ground?

So spiritual growth is really pretty simple. Stay connected to God and you'll grow. And remember that the way we stay connected is by regularly reading His Word and talking to Him and then obeying whatever it is He's telling us to do.

Wisdom will multiply your days and add years to your life.

God's Rewards

"I own all that has value and these things are Mine to give as
I choose. And My gifts are worth far more than gold; My
rewards are more valuable than money. And if you love Me,
you will inherit My treasures; I've already set up a savings
account in your name." PROVERBS 8:18-19, 21

Maybe it seems weird to think that God's going to reward
you someday. Like maybe you shouldn't be thinking
about something like that—like maybe it's selfish or shallow or
just plain wrong. But the fact is that God talks about rewarding
us—*a lot.* His Word is full of promises of rewards—both good and
bad...good for those who believe Him and obey Him, and bad
for those who don't.

And if you're reading His Word, you may be starting to
comprehend just how many rewards He has for us, not just in
heaven, but right here on earth too. Like He promises to protect us; to give us what we need; to give us good health, long life,
love, peace, joy—all kinds of really valuable things (things that
money can't buy). But in order to obtain these promises, we
need to do our part too. First, we need to keep God as our
number one priority—to love Him above all else (more than a
girlfriend or boyfriend or even our families). And then we
need to do what He asks of us—we need to stay obedient to Him.

And then, just as a generous dad likes giving nice gifts to his kids, God is even happier to give really great gifts to us. Okay, so does this mean our lives will be perfect from here on out and we'll always have everything we could ever dream of? Well, you probably already know the answer to that. Because God is God—and He knows absolutely everything about everyone (past, present, and future)—He also knows what is totally best for you. So when He gives gifts, they might not always look exactly like what they actually are. For instance, to give us the gift of patience He might need to stretch and try us a little so that we can learn how to use patience and appreciate its value. But that doesn't make it any less of a gift, does it?

And then finally the day will come when we'll get the best gift of all—eternity with God in heaven. And that'll be something completely beyond our wildest dreams—something so cool that we can't even begin to imagine it.

The reward of the godly will last. Godly people find life.

PROVERBS 11:18-19, NLT

Taking Proverbs Another Step

Hopefully by now you're feeling just a little bit intrigued by the ancient book of Proverbs. And maybe you're ready to start reading some of these Proverbs for yourself—or maybe you already have. A good plan, and one that's easy to stick to, is to read one chapter of Proverbs for each day of the month. There are thirty-one chapters, so it works out pretty well.

This plan, combined with your regular Bible reading, can really have a deep impact on your life and your thinking. And you can continue it throughout the year—reading through the whole book of Proverbs every single month.

And what's really interesting is how one or two verses will really jump out at you each time you read (don't worry if you don't get it all—no one does!). God will use these verses to guide you along throughout your day. Then in the next month, when you're reading the same chapter again, you might be drawn to a completely different verse. It's just the way God works. You might even want to keep a Proverbs journal to see how God uses the various Proverbs in your life.

Whatever you do, may God bless you abundantly, and may you always walk with Him in wisdom and in love!

Multnomah Publishers

The publisher and author would love to hear your
comments about this book. *Please contact us at:*
www.multnomah.net/piercingproverbs

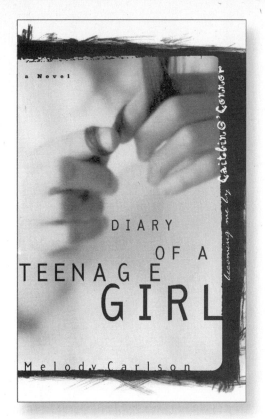

Follow Caitlin O'Conner, a girl much like you...

...as she makes her way from New Year's to the first day of summer—surviving a challenging home life, changing friends, school pressures, an identity crisis, and the uncertanties of "true love." You'll cry with Caitlin as she experiences heartache and cheer for her as she encounters a new reality in her life: God. See how rejection by one group can—incredibly—sometimes lead you to discover who you really are....

ISBN 1-57673-735-7

Caitlin's Story Continues: Her Commitment to Christ Tested by Time....

Caitlin O'Conner faces new trials as she grows in her faith and strives to maintain the recent commitments she's made to God. As a new believer, Caitlin begins her summer job and makes preparations for a Mexico mission trip with her church youth group. Torn between new spiritual directions and loyalty to Beanie, her best friend, Caitlin searches out her personal values on friendship, romance, dating, life goals, and key relationships with God and family. Her year climaxes in the realization that maturity sometimes means that life-impacting decisions must be made...by faith alone.

ISBN 1-57673-772-1

DIARY OF A TEENAGE GIRL SERIES, BOOK 3

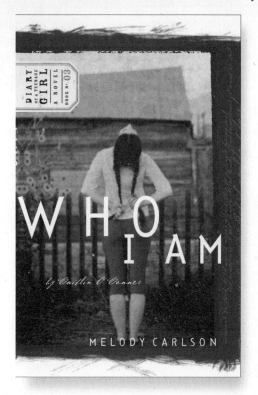

Caitlin's Search for Spirituality, Truth, and Meaning Continues...

It's challenging enough to be a normal high school senior—but Caitlin O'Conner has a host of new difficulties to deal with in the third book of Melody Carlson's widely popular and fascinating teen series. Time is critical to help the orphans in Mexico, missions-minded Caitlin believes, but Mom and Dad are set on her attending college. Meanwhile, her relationship with Josh takes on a serious tone via e-mail—threatening her commitment to "kiss dating goodbye." When Beanie begins dating an African-American, Caitlin's concern over dating seems to be misread as racism. One thing is obvious: God is at work through this dynamic girl in very real but puzzling ways. A soul-stretching time of racial reconciliation at school and within her church helps her discover God's will as never before.

ISBN 1-57673-890-6

www.letstalkfiction.com